Let's Play!

Subtraction Facts

Sara A. Johnson

Publishing Credits

Dona Herweck Rice, *Editor-in-Chief*; Lee Aucoin, *Creative Director*; Don Tran, *Print Production Manager*; Timothy J. Bradley, *Illustration Manager*; Jamey Acosta, *Assistant Editor*; Neri Garcia, *Interior Layout Designer*; Stephanie Reid, *Photo Editor*; Rachelle Cracchiolo, M.A. Ed., *Publisher*

Image Credits

Teacher Created Materials

5301 Oceanus Drive
Huntington Beach, CA 92649-1030
http://www.tcmpub.com

ISBN 978-1-4333-0420-0

© 2011 Teacher Created Materials, Inc.
Reprinted 2013

Table of Contents

Games in the City

Do you like to play games? Kids everywhere like to play games.

Take a walk in the **city**. You may
see a lot of kids playing games.

Many games use **subtraction**.
Subtraction is used when players get
"out." Subtraction is also used when
things are taken away.

These kids are playing checkers.
One boy started with 12 checkers.
Then he lost 9 checkers. That means
he has 3 checkers left.

$$12 - 9 = 3$$

Jump Rope

Lots of kids like to jump rope. You can play by yourself.

You can play with friends.

Some kids use 2 ropes. This is called Double Dutch.

LET'S EXPLORE MATH

There were 4 kids jumping inside the Double Dutch ropes. Then 2 kids jumped out. How many kids were left jumping?

Hopscotch

To play hopscotch, all you need is chalk and a rock.

First you throw the rock.
Then you jump. Do not jump
in the space with the rock!

Marbles

Kids like to play marbles. First draw a circle on the ground with chalk.

Then put small marbles in the circle. Use a big marble to shoot the small marbles out. This is subtraction in action!

LET'S EXPLORE MATH

There are 10 marbles in the circle. If you shoot out 2 marbles with your turn, how many marbles are left in the circle?

Then **count** what you have won.

Who won more marbles?
How do you know?

Tag

Tag is a fun game to play. You have to run fast so you do not get tagged.

You can play tag anywhere in the city. But it is not safe to play in the street.

LET'S EXPLORE MATH

There were 11 kids playing a game of tag. Then 5 kids got tagged. How many kids were left playing the game?

Handball

If you have a rubber ball and a wall, you can play handball. You need 2 or more people to play this game.

Put your hand in a fist. Then hit the ball against the wall. You can only let the ball bounce 1 time or you are out.

Basketball

There are many basketball **courts** in the city.

You can play with your friends.

LET'S EXPLORE MATH

There were 14 kids playing basketball. Then 6 kids had to go home for dinner. How many kids were left playing the game?

All you need is a basketball and a hoop.

These kids keep score in their game.
They use a chalkboard.

Team A has 11 points. Team B has
7 points. Team A has 4 more points
than Team B.

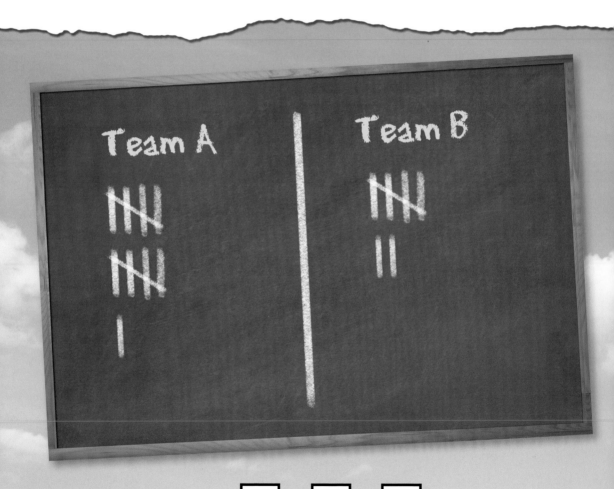

$$11 - 7 = 4$$

Soccer

Soccer is a game that kids play in countries all over the world.

Cambodia

Africa

Iraq

You can not use your hands in this game. You can only kick the ball with your feet.

Go Play!

There are many fun games to play in the city. Get your friends and go play!

Buying Toys

Cole has been saving his allowance. He wants to buy a gift for his sister. He also wants to buy something for himself. Cole has $15.00. He buys a jump rope for his sister. It costs $4.00. He buys some trading cards for himself. They cost $3.00. How much money does Cole have left?

Solve It!

Use the steps below to help you solve the problem.

Step 1: Subtract the cost of the jump rope from the amount of money Cole has.

Step 2: Write down that number.

Step 3: Subtract the cost of the trading cards from the new amount left over. That is how much Cole has left after buying both items.

$3.00

Glossary

city—a busy town where a lot of people live and work

count—to name or list the units of a group one by one in order to determine a total

courts—areas for playing sports

Double Dutch—a jump rope game in which players jump over 2 ropes

street—a public road where cars and other vehicles are driven

subtraction—the process of finding the difference between 2 numbers

team—a group of people who work or play a game together

Index

Let's Explore Math

Page 10:
2 kids left

Page 14:
8 marbles left

Page 17:
6 kids left

Page 21:
8 kids left

Solve the Problem

$15.00 – $4.00 = $11.00
$11.00 – $3.00 = $8.00
Cole has $8.00 left.